The Truth About Teachers

Paul, David, Brian and Roger are not only fantastic bestselling poets. They are fantastic bestselling poets with inside information. Once upon a time they were all teachers . . . so they know all about teachers and their secrets. If you like, they could come to your school, perform their poems AND tell you the secrets that weren't allowed in this book.

David Parkins has illustrated numerous books, ranging from maths textbooks to the *Beano*. His picture books have been shortlisted for the Smarties Book Prize and the Kurt Maschler Award. He lives in Canada with his wife, three children and six cats.

D1471810

Also available from Macmillan Children's Books

The Truth about Parents
*Hilarious Rhymes by Paul Cookson, David Harmer,
Brian Moses and Roger Stevens*

It's Behind You!
Monster poems by Paul Cookson and David Harmer

It Came from Outer Space!
Poems by Paul Cookson and David Harmer

Spill the Beans
Poems by Paul Cookson and David Harmer

Olympic Poems (100% Unofficial)
By Brian Moses and Roger Stevens

Pants on Fire
Poems by Paul Cookson

Pirate Poems
By David Harmer

Behind the Staffroom Door
The Very Best of Brian Moses

A Cat Called Elvis
Brilliant poems by Brian Moses

Why Otters Don't Wear Socks
Poems by Roger Stevens

How to Embarrass Teachers
Poems chosen by Paul Cookson

Aliens Stole My Underpants
Alien poems chosen by Brian Moses

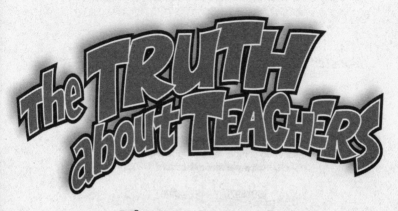

Hilarious Rhymes by
Paul Cookson, David Harmer,
Brian Moses and Roger Stevens

Illustrated by
David Parkins

MACMILLAN CHILDREN'S BOOKS

This book is for all teachers – the teachers who taught us, the teachers we taught with, the teachers we meet on our travels and all the teachers teaching in schools today. Very best wishes, Paul, David, Brian and Roger

First published 2007 by Macmillan Children's Books

This edition published 2013 by Macmillan Children's Books
a division of Macmillan Publishers Limited
20 New Wharf Road, London N1 9RR
Basingstoke and Oxford
Associated companies throughout the world
www.panmacmillan.com

ISBN 978-1-4472-4214-7

Text copyright © Paul Cookson, David Harmer,
Brian Moses and Roger Stevens 2007
Illustrations copyright © David Parkins 2007

The right of Paul Cookson, David Harmer, Brian Moses, Roger Stevens and
David Parkins to be identified as the authors and illustrator of this work has been asserted
by them in accordance with the Copyright, Designs and Patents Act 1988.

1 3 5 7 9 8 6 4 2

A CIP catalogue record for this book is available from the British Library.

Typeset by Tony Fleetwood
Printed and bound by CPI Group (UK) Ltd, Croydon CR0 4YY

Contents

Teachers – *Roger Stevens* 1

Mister Moore – *David Harmer* 3

What Mr Kenning Does When He Thinks
　We Aren't Looking – *Paul Cookson* 6

From the Photo Galleries in School Entrance Halls: 1. Mrs Smellie,
　2. Miss Vicious, 3. Miss Fish, 4. Mrs Jolly, 5. Mr Batty,
　6. Mrs Slaughter – *Brian Moses* 8

Gooooaaaaalllll!!!!! – *Roger Stevens* 14

Mrs Eagle's Eyes – *Paul Cookson* 16

Mr Phillipson's Rubber Face – *Paul Cookson* 18

Me! I Teach PE – *Paul Cookson* 20

Middle Names – *Brian Moses* 22

Teacher Translations – *Paul Cookson* 24

A Televised Surprise – *David Harmer* 26

The Estuary Field Trip – *Roger Stevens* 27

A Sea Creature Ate Our Teacher – *Brian Moses* 28

We Lost Our Teacher to the Sea – *David Harmer* 30

The Secret Diary of Miss – Aged 24 – *Paul Cookson* 32

New Neighbours – *David Harmer* 33

Assembly Song – *Roger Stevens* 34

Introducing Dad – *Roger Stevens* 35

Silent Reading – *Roger Stevens* 36

We're Staying Here! – *Roger Stevens* 37

A Surprise for Year Five – *David Harmer* 38

Visitors Beware! It's the Secret Staffroom Chair! – *Paul Cookson* . 41

Cakes in the Staffroom – *Brian Moses* 42

The Secret Life of Mr Sibson – *Paul Cookson* 44

Mr Charmer's Ear – *Paul Cookson* 46

Teacher on a Bike – *Roger Stevens* 49

A Story of Snowballs – *David Harmer* 50

Our New Teacher – *Roger Stevens* 52

A Deadly Secret – *David Harmer* 53

A Letter from the New Head Teacher – *Paul Cookson*......... 55

It's a Definite Sign – *Paul Cookson* 56

The Lone Teacher – *David Harmer*......................... 57

Why Miss Needs a Bigger Wardrobe Than Sir – *Paul Cookson* ... 58

Mr Pyewipe's Assembly – *David Harmer*.................... 59

Strange Hobbies – *Brian Moses* 61

Teachers' Playtime – *Roger Stevens*...................... 62

Mr Walton's on the Playground – *Roger Stevens*............. 64

Help! – *David Harmer* 65

A Letter to the Teacher – *David Harmer*................... 67

A Spell to Make the Headmaster's Trousers Fall Down
   During Assembly – *David Harmer* 68

Our Teacher Is Really from Outer Space – *David Harmer*...... 70

I've Seen Mrs Newton's Knickers – *Paul Cookson* 72

An Infant's Eye View of Teachers – *Paul Cookson* 74

Teacher's Pet – *Roger Stevens* 75

Our Teacher – *Brian Moses*.............................. 77

Sheep Wars: the Drama Teacher's Dilemma! – *Brian Moses* 78

Teacher's Desk – *Roger Stevens*......................... 79

Not to Be Crossed (a sonnet) – *Roger Stevens*............... 80

SATs for Teachers – *David Harmer*........................ 83

How Teachers Leave School Each Evening – *Brian Moses* 85

Teachers' Awards – *Brian Moses* 87

What Miss Did on Her Last Day in School – *Paul Cookson* 89

Teachers

Teachers are happy
All of the while
Teachers are cheery
Teachers all smile
Teachers have eyes
In the back of their heads
Teachers remember
The good things you said
Teachers are friendly
Teachers are kind
Teachers can always
See into your mind

1

Teachers will help
If you're stuck with your sums
Teachers like stillness
But not wriggle-bums
Teachers are visitors
From outer space
Teachers play Scrabble
But never kiss chase
Teachers like writing
Their writing is neat
Teachers are honest
Teachers don't cheat
Teachers walk or ride bikes
(They don't have much choice
They can't afford cars
And they'd love a Rolls-Royce)
Teachers eat salad
And stinky old cheese
Teachers have patches on jackets
And knees
Teachers are fair
Though they can give cross looks
Teachers have hobbies
They love marking books
I'm glad I'm a teacher
The best in the town
now open your books
Be quiet
And SIT DOWN!

Roger Stevens

Mister Moore

Mister Moore, Mister Moore
Creaking down the corridor.

Uh uh eh eh uh
Uh uh eh eh uh

Mister Moore wears wooden suits
Mister Moore's got great big boots
Mister Moore's got hair like a brush
And Mister Moore don't like me much.

Mister Moore, Mister Moore
Creaking down the corridor.

Uh uh eh eh uh
Uh uh eh eh uh

When my teacher's there I haven't got a care
I can do my sums, I can do gerzinters
When Mister Moore comes through the door
Got a wooden head filled with splinters.

Mister Moore, Mister Moore
Creaking down the corridor.

Uh uh eh eh uh
Uh uh eh eh uh

Mister Moore, I implore
My ear-holes ache, my head is sore
Don't come through that classroom door.
Don't come through that classroom door.

Mister Moore, Mister Moore
Creaking down the corridor.

Uh uh eh eh uh
Uh uh eh eh uh

Big voice big hands
Big voice he's a very big man
Take my advice, be good be very very nice
Be good be very very nice
To Mister Moore, Mister Moore
Creaking down the corridor.

Uh uh eh eh uh
Uh uh eh eh uh

Mister Moore wears wooden suits
Mister Moore's got great big boots
Mister Moore's got hair like a brush
Mister Moore don't like me much.

Mister Moore, Mister Moore
Creaking down the corridor.

Uh uh eh eh uh
Uh uh eh eh uh

David Harmer

What Mr Kenning Does When He Thinks We Aren't Looking

Space gazer
Nostril wrinkler
Idle doodler
Paper crinkler

Tie fiddler
Fly checker
Blu-Tack moulder
Paper-clip wrecker

Pen-top sucker
Teeth grinder
Fingernail nibbler
Watch winder

Rubber sniffer
Pencil roller
Song hummer
iPod scroller

Burp stifler
Eye closer
Paper reader
Nearly dozer

Ear-hole cleaner
Fluff flicker
Toffee chewer
Nose picker

Paul Cookson

6

mmm-
mmm

TOFFEE

From the Photo Galleries in School Entrance Halls

1. Mrs Smellie

Mrs Smellie
is a bit
of a
misnomer.
She's a perfume
fanatic
who loves
the aroma
of lavender
one day,
violets
another,
but we really
wouldn't
want any
other.
She's tulips
in spring,
she's summer
come early,
an oasis
of calm
in the hurly-
burly,
in the rough
and tumble
of life
at our school,
Mrs Smellie
is unbelievably
cool.

8

2. Miss Vicious

Miss Vicious
is not
at all
what
you might
expect
from
a name
like hers.
She's really
fun
and when
we do
good work
Miss Vicious
purrrrrrrrs!

3. Miss Fish

If I only had one wish
it would be for me
to stay with
Miss Fish
forever
and float
in warm
Caribbean
seas,
feeling
the breath
of a light
sea breeze.
For that's
how
Miss Fish
makes
me feel,
and I wonder
sometimes
if she's real.
Lovely Miss Fish,
such a
heavenly creature,
an angelfish
sort of
teacher.

4. Mrs Jolly

You could hang
a sprig of holly
on Mrs Jolly.
She's Christmas
all year round,
the very best
present
you've ever
found
beneath your
Christmas tree.
Her smile
has the sparkle
of snow
in the sun,
she's every
game that
you've ever
won.
Never too
busy
to stop
and play,
Mrs Jolly
is everyone's
Christmas
Day.

5. Mr Batty

Arthur
Reginald
William
Batty
is one
of the
strange
ones,
really
scatty.
Anything
can make
him
ratty,
other
times
he's
really
chatty.
Makes
remarks
that are
sometimes
catty,
wears
a suit
that's really
natty.
One of
the
strange
ones
is
Arthur
Batty.

12

6. Mrs Slaughter

Everyone knows
about Mrs Slaughter,
but for any new pupils
we feel we oughta
warn you how
with one mistake
you'll make Mrs Slaughter
tremble and shake.
You oughta be careful,
you oughta take care
not to get
in Mrs Slaughter's hair.
Don't get under her feet
or up her nose
or quickly she will
metamorphose
into something you
just won't want to know,
she'll simply become
your deadliest foe.
So now you know
just what to expect
if you fail to give
Mrs Slaughter respect.

Brian Moses

GOOOOAAAAALLLLLL!!!!!

I run rings round Ronny
I'm clever and fast
I sell Sal a dummy
With a twinkle I'm past

I weave
I dive
I tackle
I spin
And no one can catch me
I'm a whirlwind

Then I pass every player
You all know my name!
I'm Joe Cole, I'm Rooney
I'm the best in the game

The ball's on my head
The ball's on my boot
I bamboozle the goalie
I dummy, I shoot

Darren dives –
It's a gooooaaaaallllll!!!!!
It's a total sensation!
And I dance
Round the corner flag
In celebration

now it's our turn, says Billy
You've had the ball long enough
I say, Hey!
I'm the teacher
If you don't like it – Tough!

Roger Stevens

Mrs Eagle's Eyes

Eyes, eyes – Mrs Eagle's eyes
Eyes, eyes – Mrs Eagle's eyes
Sharpened beak, taloned claws
Strutting down the corridors
Eyes, eyes – Mrs Eagle's eyes

Hypnotizing, mesmerizing, traumatizing, most surprising
Magnifying, terrifying, spying, prying, mystifying
Scary eyes, starey eyes, ever watchful wary eyes

Eyes, eyes . . .

X-ray eyes, death-ray eyes, scanning every which way eyes
Beady eyes, speedy eyes, greedy, needy, seedy eyes
Laser eyes, razor eyes, amazing in their gazing eyes

Eyes, eyes . . .

There's nothing you can hide from – Mrs Eagle's eyes
When they are open wide – Mrs Eagle's eyes
Watching like a hawk – Mrs Eagle's eyes
Nobody dare talk – Mrs Eagle's eyes
Everything she sees – Mrs Eagle's eyes
Three sixty degrees – Mrs Eagle's eyes

Eyes, eyes . . .

Paul Cookson

16

Mr Phillipson's Rubber Face

He looks normal . . . most of the time
but occasionally he can transform his face amazingly.

It's really funny . . . most of the time
but sometimes he does it to get his own back.

Like . . . in the head teacher's serious assembly,
or during a silent test

Or even worse . . .
just when Mrs Mountain the dinner lady is walking past.

He times it perfectly
so that only the children can see him.

He can make his eyeballs disappear
and touch his Adam's apple with his tongue,

Inflate his nostrils to twice their normal size
and twitch his nostril hairs so that they dance,

Wiggle his ears and join his eyebrows together
while stretching his neck so the veins stand out.

He can do aliens, monsters, Halloween masks,
most of the pupils and staff.

He can even do the dinner lady and the head teacher
. . . at the same time.

But the trick is this.
He only does them for a split second.

Just long enough for us to see.
Just long enough to make us laugh out loud in the silence.

And that's when we get told off.
And that's when he smiles to himself.

Paul Cookson

Me! I Teach PE

Me! I teach PE
Not history or geography, maths or English or RE
PE! That's me!
Not chemistry, biology, physics, drama, CDT
PE! That's me!
Not French or German, PSE or soci-poncy-ology
PE! That's me!

The subject of the gods – because it's taught by me
Bronzed and bold and beautiful – me! I teach PE!

Whatever the weather is weather for sports
Football pitch or tennis courts
All year round I wear my shorts
I write one sentence on reports.

A mine of sporting general knowledge
Go on ask me who
Scored the winner in the FA Cup of seventy-two.
Who scored the only single try at Twickers eighty-three?
I'll tell you what and where and why cos me I teach PE.

Watch *A Question of Sport* on BBC
PE! That's me!
The midweek match on ITV
PE! That's me!
Permanent action – BSkyB
PE! That's me!

I don't like fat kids, don't like weeds
Pigeon toes or knobbly knees
Kids in glasses, kids who wheeze
Do not give me wimps like these!

Sport's the only crucial thing
Numero Uno – that is me
PE Rules and I am King
The man in charge – I teach PE.

It's great to teach this subject
I know I teach it well
It's great to teach a subject
That even I can spell . . .

P – E – That's me!

Paul Cookson

Middle Names

Do you know your teacher's middle name?

Would it be one that they'd be
too embarrassed to reveal?

Maybe it's something potty like Dotty
or silly like Chantilly,
something divine like Columbine
or medicinal like Calomine,
something modern like Ikea
or historical like Boadicea.

Perhaps it's something seasonal
like Primrose,
or a name that gets up your nose
like Hyacinth.

Maybe it's American like Hank
or solid and British like Frank.
Maybe it's barbaric like Conan
or boy-bandish and poppy
like Ronan.

Perhaps it's old fashioned
like Dora and Norah,
or something buttery
like Flora.

Maybe it's expensive like Pearl
or with a country twang like Merle.
Is it something classy like Clancy
or fancy like Nancy,
something Biblical like Zachariah,
Amos, Moses or Jeremiah?

Is it witchy like Winnie
or moany like Minnie,
sensible like Fred,
countrified like Ned?

Is it tragic like Romeo
or Italian like Antonio?

Is it Zebedee or Gertrude,
Marvin or Ermintrude?
Is it Cecil or Boris,
Marmaduke or Doris?

Now go spread rumours
all round school.
Your teachers have names
that just aren't cool.

It's sure to embarrass them!

Brian Moses

Teacher Translations

We'll go over that tomorrow
I haven't learned that bit yet

I wanted to take my time and mark your projects objectively
I've lost them

The caretaker locked your work in a cupboard before half-term
I've lost those as well

Come on, you guys – we have to do literacy and numeracy
Yes, I know they're boring

It is the head teacher's job to take assembly
Yes, that's boring as well

Tomorrow we have some special visitors who will be
watching us
*Tomorrow we've got the nasty OFSTED inspectors trying to
catch me out*

My class has visitors
My class has nits

There are some characters in our year
I can only think of naughty words to describe them

I think you deserve a longer afternoon playtime today
*I really need three cups of coffee, a chocolate rush and some
headache pills*

It's not my time we are wasting, I don't mind how long we wait here.
When we are all ready, we can come back later and practise all
this in your own time
I can't think of anything else to say

Paul Cookson

24

FUN! FUN! FUN!

(Boring! Boring! Boring!)

A Televised Surprise

Imagine our delight
Consternation and surprise
Our teacher on *Come Dancing*
Right before our eyes.

She wore a dress of sequins
That glittered like a flight
Of silent, silver snowflakes
On a winter's night.

She really looked fantastic
No one could ignore
The magic of her dancing
Across the ballroom floor.

Her partner, tall and smart
Only saw him from the back,
Oily hair slicked down short
His suit and shoes were black.

He whirled and twirled her round
As the music got much faster
And then he faced the camera
It was our headmaster!

They seemed to dance forever
Until it wasn't fun
And then the competition stopped
The pair of them had won.

David Harmer

The Estuary Field Trip

I walked with my class along the estuary
The salty wind sneaked through the cracked concrete
of time-worn sea defences,
stirred the weeds and rusty wire
that criss-crossed the caked mud bed
Thirty children poked under rocks
hunting for crabs
and tugged at a limp of driftwood,
perhaps once part of a sailing barge
taking bricks to London

Isn't it beautiful, I said
Richard looked up at me, nodded, smiled
A rare moment
A mystical union of teacher and pupil
Mr Stevens, he said,
did you see the Man U game last night?

Roger Stevens

A Sea Creature Ate Our Teacher

Our teacher said that it's always good
to have an inquisitive mind,
then he told us, 'Go check the rock pools,
let's see what the tide's left behind.'

The muscles on his arms were bulging
as he pushed rocks out of the way
'Identify what you see,' he called
'Note it down in your book straight away.'

It was just as he spoke when we smelt it,
a stench, like something rotten,
a wobbling mass of wet black skin
like something time had forgotten.

In front of us, snaking up from the pool,
was a hideous slime-soaked creature
with a huge black hole of a mouth
that vacuumed up our teacher.

I didn't actually see him go,
I was looking away at the time,
but I saw two legs sticking out
and trainers covered in slime.

But our teacher must have given this creature
such chronic indigestion.
It found out soon that to try and digest him
was simply out of the question.

28

It gave an almighty lunge of its neck
and spat our teacher out.
He was spread with the most revolting goo
and staggering about.

None of us moved to help him
as he wiped the gunge from his head.
We looked at each other and smirked.
'That'll teach *him* a lesson,' we said!

Brian Moses

We Lost Our Teacher to the Sea

We've been at the seaside all day
collecting shells, drawing the view
doing science in the rock pools.

Our teacher went to find the sea's edge
and stayed there, he's sitting on a rock
he won't come back.

His glasses are frosted over with salt
his beard has knotted into seaweed
his black suit is covered in limpets.

He's staring into the wild water
singing to the waves
sharing a joke with the herring gulls.

We sent out the coastguard
the lifeboat and the orange helicopter
he told them all to go away.

We're getting on the bus with our sticks of rock
our presents for Mum
and our jotters and pencils.

He's still out there as we leave
arms out stretched to the pale blue sky
the tide racing towards him.

His slippery fishtail flaps
with a flick and a shimmer he's gone
back to the sea forever.

David Harmer

30

The Secret Diary of Miss – Aged 24

The day she left her desk unlocked,
The things we saw inside . . .
Perfume, blusher, red lipgloss,
A diary she'd tried to hide.

The pages just fell open (honest) . . .

Monday	Mr C
Tuesday	Mr Jackson
Wednesday	Mr B
Thursday	Mr Lawrence
Friday	Mr Best
Saturday night	Mr Wright
Sunday	. . . have a rest!

Then in red she'd written comments,
What she really thought.
She'd given all these teachers
And their features a report . . .

Mr C is coarse and vulgar and could do much better
Mr Jackson tries too hard and thinks he's a trend setter
Mr B is really creepy and he thinks he's cool
Mr Lawrence won't shut up and only talks of school
Mr Best was just the worst – a poser and a big-head
Mr Wright was dull and trite and never heard a word I said.

All of them just waste my time, it felt just like detention.
None of them can make a mark deserving my attention.
None of them can pass my test, all fail miserably.
None of them will get a note saying, 'Please see me.'

Paul Cookson

32

New Neighbours

Living next door to my head teacher isn't easy.

I couldn't believe it when he moved in
Mum laughed, said it didn't matter
I only had Year Six to go
so what?

I can still hear him
booming out all over the garden
as he tells the bushes off for being untidy
shouts at the flowers to stand up straight
yells at the starlings to sing in tune
commands the lawn to get itself cut
gives the sparrows lines for being cheeky.

Yesterday I felt
his bulging eyes stare at me and Smigsy
playing football in the garden.
He disallowed three of my goals
sent Smigsy home for answering back
then he confiscated our ball
when it bounced on his head
and flattened his hollyhocks.

Mum says I'm over-reacting
it's not all that bad, and he has banned me
from riding my bike outside his front window
it'll teach me a lesson in manners.

She must be joking, and what's worse
is that the house on the other side is up for sale
and we've been told
the senior dinner lady is going to live there.
Mum, please, when can we move?
I can't take much more of this.

David Harmer

33

AssemBly Song

Dance, dance,
Wherever you may be
I am the Lord of the Dark Settee
and I'll bounce on you
and you can bounce on me
and we'll all sit down
and watch TV

Roger Stevens

Introducing Dad

If I may, Miss
I'd like to introduce my dad
Mum left us last year
And that made him really sad
He told me you were pretty
And his favourite colour's beige
And it isn't that uncommon
To date women half your age
And we all know that he's bald
Beneath that funny flick of hair
You just have to humour him
And pretend his hair's all there
His feet smell a bit funny
And his brain's a trifle slow
And you haven't got a boyfriend, Miss
So . . . could you please give Dad a go?

Roger Stevens

35

Silent Reading

Teacher says,
Sit down!
Be quiet!
Take out your reading books!
Read silently!

Then he puts
His feet up
Reads
The *Beano*
Drinks his tea

Roger Stevens

We're Staying Here!

We don't care if there's a riot
And 4A are fighting 4B
We're staying here in the staffroom
It's a civilized place to be

Don't care if Ken's locked in the cupboard
And Sammy has swallowed the key
We're staying here in the staffroom
As cosy as can be

Don't care if Randeep has thrown up
Or Belinda's been stung by a bee
We're staying here in the staffroom
Watching the match on TV

Don't care if Sammy has stolen Neil's pants
And hung them up in a tree
We're staying here in the staffroom
Drinking cups of tea

For here in the staffroom everything's calm
And there's peace and harmony
And we're staying here every day from now on
From nine until half past three

Roger Stevens

37

A Surprise for Year Five

Mr Grindleford came to school
Extra early this morning
Rubbing his hands and wearing a smile
He started his work for the day ahead.

He put two mice in Hannah's drawer
Four more in Jake's, seven in Kevin's
He found Kyle's coat still there on the peg
Poured wallpaper paste into the hood
Then filled the pockets with worms and spiders.
He cut through the legs of Jonathan's chair
To catch him out when he swings backwards
Dripped treacle and syrup over Karim's work
Poured engine oil into his book bag.
He stuck slugs and snails on all the paint trays
Wrote rude rhymes over the board
Popped open a mousetrap on Jennifer's chair
Smeared superglue over the others
He hid whoopee cushions and drawing pins
Under the seats in the reading corner
Filled the waste-paper basket up with frogs
And balanced a bucket of paint on the door.
Just as his class walked up the path
He pushed the clock forwards so they would be late.

Mr Grindleford opened the storeroom
And settling down with the paper and pencils
Like a hidden tiger ready to pounce
He waited for the screaming to start.

David Harmer

Visitors Beware! It's the Secret Staffroom Chair!

In the corner of the staffroom,
well worn and threadbare –
the booby-trapped, elastic-snapped,
collapsing secret chair.
Teachers leave it well alone,
they know what's lurking there . . .
the buttock-clenching, jacket-wrenching
never-mentioned chair.

The only seat that's left at break
so trying to relax
you sink in the ever-shrinking
chair apt to collapse.
Your coffee cup shoots ten feet up,
your knees are in your hair
in the folding, overloading,
self-imploding chair.

When sitting with the teachers
all visitors beware –
the jacket-wrenching, buttock-clenching,
ever-sinking, ever-shrinking,
self-imploding, overloading,
parping, squeaking, trouser-tweaking,
twisting, turning, non-discerning,
living, breathing, most deceiving,
booby-trapped, elastic-snapped,
collapsing staffroom chair.

Paul Cookson

41

Cakes in the Staffroom

Nothing gets teachers more excited
than cakes in the staffroom at break-time.
Nothing gets them more delighted
than the sight of plates
piled high with jammy doughnuts
or chocolate cake.

It's an absolute stampede
as the word gets round quickly,

And it's, 'Oooh, these are really delicious,'
and, 'Aaah, these doughnuts are ace.'

And you hear them say, 'I really shouldn't,'
or, 'Just a tiny bit, I'm on a diet.'

Really, it's the only time they're quiet
when they're cramming cakes into their mouths,
when they're wearing a creamy moustache
or the jam squirts out like blood,
or they're licking chocolate
from their fingers.

You can tell when they've been scoffing,
they get lazy in literacy,
sleepy in silent reading,
nonsensical in numeracy,
and look guilty in assembly.

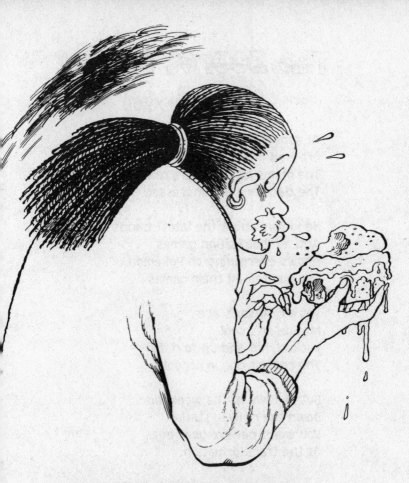

But nothing gets teachers more excited
than cakes in the staffroom at break-time,
unless of course
it's wine in the staffroom at lunchtime!

Brian Moses

The Secret Life of Mr Sibson

At school he's just the coolest teacher
Dressed in his designer best
The mums all think he's really great
The dads are not impressed.

He knows about the latest bands
And all PlayStation games
Knows everything on Pokémon,
Can you tell all their names.

Yes Mr Sibson's ace
Mr Sibson's cool
Wicked, hip and up to date
The coolest guy in school.

But see him at the weekend
Down the railway station
You won't believe your eyes
At the transformation.

A knitted blue and yellow scarf
An orange large cagoule
A pair of flares, brown corduroy . . .
He doesn't seem so cool.

A duffel bag that's stuffed with crisps
A pair of thick-rimmed glasses
Binoculars for peering at
Any train that passes.

A thousand pens for writing down
The numbers in his jotter
Mr Sibson's secret . . .
He's really a trainspotter.

Paul Cookson

Mr Charmer's Ear

I couldn't believe it when Mum told me.
Said she'd seen him in Our Price records,
browsing through the Rolling Stones and Bob Dylan sections.
I mean, he is our head teacher
and he must be nearly fifty . . . at least.

I couldn't believe it when Mum told me.
About Mr Charmer's ear . . .
and the new addition.
He can't have, just can't have,
not at his age . . .

I couldn't believe it when Mum told me.
Mr Charmer's got an earring,
a great big dangly silver one with a cross and feather on.

But when Mum told me
that he daren't wear it for school
in case he gets told off by the dinner ladies,
well, I could believe that.

Everyone's frightened of *them*.

Paul Cookson

Teacher on a Bike

We go to school in the people carrier
And I like it
Our teacher hasn't got a people carrier
Or a car
Our teacher has to bike it

She says a bike is brilliant
She says a bike is *brill*
It's fun on a bike, our teacher says
Until you go up a hill
It's fun on a bike
It's . . . fun . . . on . . . a . . . bike
It's . . . . . . fun . . . . . . on . . . . . . a . . . . . . bike . . . . . .
Until . . .
You . . .
Go . . .
Up . . .

A . . .

Hill . . .

But-a-bike's-a-wonderful-thing-to-ride
Comingdownontheotherside

Roger Stevens

49

A Story of Snowballs

Only last week down by the canal
I met Shiner Smith, my very best pal
A cold winter's day filled up with snow
The water was grey, the going was slow.

We both felt so bored, there was nothing to do
But then a small pleasure craft chugged into view
A big man with a beard was steering the boat
Wrapped up in a scarf and a thick overcoat.

Shiner looked hard at this nautical bloke
Said 'Let's chuck him a snowball, just for a joke'.
'You what?' I replied. 'You wouldn't dare'
But one had already whizzed through the air!

So I scraped up some snow hard in my fist
The boat hardly moved, it couldn't be missed
I gave the packed snowball one final squeeze
Then shouted 'Oy, Fatty, have one of these!'

He was so angry, red-faced and sore
He felt even worse when we threw twenty more
He shouted 'Hey, stop that. Just pack it in!'
Got splattered by Shiner smack on the chin.

I landed a beauty right down his neck
Another one burst like a bomb on his deck
He slipped on the bits, lost his footing and fell
Bounced like a ball and gave a loud yell.

We lobbed him some others, ran from the path
Into the woods and had a good laugh
Then we said goodbye and soon forgot
About our sad sailor and the soaking he got.

Several days later school started again
I was feeling OK, so was Shiner, but when
We walked through the gate and over the yard
We noticed our teacher glaring quite hard.

Beside him there stood a man that we knew
Last time we'd seen him he'd turned the air blue
Shouting and yelling through a big beard
I started to feel shaky and weird.

He snarled 'Glad to meet you. Just couldn't wait
I'm your new headteacher, I'm Mr Tate
So you like to play snowballs?' he said with a sneer
'Well I'd like to have a word in your ear.

'I hope you enjoyed your moment of fun
Just phoned your parents to say what you've done
But this time, my friends, it's my turn to win
In fact, here they are! Come in! Let's begin!'

David Harmer

Our New Teacher

Last Christmas our teacher went skiing
Leaping from glaciers with glee
She zoomed down ravines like a champion
But she couldn't get on with 6B

At Easter she sailed around Iceland
Pitting her wits 'gainst the sea
She rode the huge waves single-handed
But she just couldn't handle 6B

In summer she went pony-trekking
Through the wild mountain ranges of Chile
Went white-water rafting in a tiny canoe
But she couldn't cope with 6B

Now 6B have left for the big school
And teacher has us in her charge
And we love to hear her adventures
And we're all well behaved – by and large

So we asked, Do you miss your old class, Miss?
And she went all quiet and sad
Then her face lit up and she started to laugh
What, me? Miss 6B? Are you mad?

Roger Stevens

A Deadly Secret

Our new teacher scares us stiff
one glare from his big red eyes
you don't move, one poke
from his long, bony fingers
you stand still, one chilly blast
of his icy breath down your neck
you're frozen to the spot.

At first we thought he was ill
his saggy face, all pale and grey
and that his uncanny resemblance
to the portrait in the hall
of the school's first head teacher
painted in 1922
was just a coincidence.

Then he began to howl and gibber
during assembly, started to float
along the corridor a metre off the ground
arrived each morning
wrapped in a long heavy chain
made of school bells, registers and Ofsted reports.

Yesterday we finally got it
when he walked through the classroom door
five minutes after it was shut
drifted through two desks and cupboard
and stood in front of the blackboard
suddenly we all saw through him

(we could read the date on the board
as well as the list of spellings for homework)
and we realized
our teacher wasn't as lively as most
our teacher was, in fact, a gh-aaaaaaaaaaaaaaagh!

David Harmer

A Letter from the New Head Teacher

Dear Parent/Guardian

As from next week we are making a few adjustments to the school uniform.

All pupils must wear the following:

Yellow blazers with purple polka dots
Lime-green nylon shirts
Purple velvet shorts, or
Pleated lemon skirts

Blue school tie with pink school crest
Knee-length socks of brown
New school woollen balaclava
With fluffy pompoms hanging down

It is expected that all boys
Must wear skirts that reach below the knee
And that girls' shorts must be loose
Comfortable and baggy.

Yours sincerely,

Ella Villcow

Mrs E. Villcow

Paul Cookson

55

It's a Definite Sign

Our dinner lady Mrs Mack
Is well in love with Mr Fipps
Because at every dinner-time
She winks and smiles when he's in line
And gives him extra chips.

Paul Cookson

The Lone Teacher

We've got a new teacher
he wears a mask
and a big wide hat.

He comes to school
on a silver horse
and rides around the field
all day.

Sometimes he says
'Have you seen Toronto?'

We tell him
we haven't been to Canada
but it is near
the Panama Canal
we did that in geography
last term.

At four o'clock
he rides off into the sunset
and comes back the next morning
in a cloud of dust.

We wonder if
he will ever come and teach us maths
like he said he would
when he first arrived.

Perhaps then he'll tell us his name
not keep it a secret
because my dad always asks me
'Who is that man?'

David Harmer

57

Why Miss Needs a Bigger Wardrobe Than Sir

Men . . . thirty years in the same suit,
Brown or grey and the same three ties,
Leather elbow patches,
A growing option with each increasing year.

Women . . . different outfits every day,
Different colours for different occasions,
Different combinations for different seasons,
Always something new.

Paul Cookson

Mr Pyewipe's Assembly

If I close my eyes
The head teacher won't notice
I'm right at the back behind Year Six
And he's droning on
About his caravan in Cleethorpes
Where even though it rained for a year
And a plague of dragons, sea monsters and jellyfish
Invaded the site
He and Mrs Head Teacher, Gertie
Had a wonderful holiday.

I've closed my eyes
I'm flying through a deep blue sky
The town below looks like a map
What's that I see?
Bearded bad-guys robbing a bank
Blazing guns, sirens howling
Good job I'm a superhero
Pieman to the rescue!
Down I zoom, my piecrust cape
Stretches out behind me
I zap the baddies with my pies
Splatter! Splosh! Spladiddle! Spladoosh!
That's got them, they've surrendered
Here comes the Queen to give me a medal!
But look, the boss of the bad-men's escaping
I'll jump on his head from this rooftop
Ker-Zappo! Ker-Zonk! Ker-Splatto!

I've opened my eyes
Oh dear, I seem to be on the floor
Wrestling with Josh out of Year Six
Everyone's laughing except the head teacher
Who's frowning an enormous frown
Perhaps it's all part of my dream
I'll give him a poke to see if it's true
Badoosh! Bosh-Bosh! Bing-Bang!
Oh dear, I seem to have thumped the head teacher
He's sitting beside me, looking quite angry
I think this might be the end of Pieman
Goodbye.

David Harmer

Strange Hobbies

Most teachers have hobbies like snooker or tennis,
or they take up jogging, or like baking cakes,
or messing with cars, or they play for a team,
or they go out sailing on lakes.
But we must have the oddest teachers,
whose hobbies are definitely weird.
Our headteacher, for example,
practises topiary* on his beard.
Mr Smith likes manicuring elephants,
Miss Tompkins builds sculptures with soap.
Mrs Dean plays tunes on fruit machines,
Mr Simms juggles telescopes.
There's nothing Mrs Grant doesn't know
about the common toenail and how it grows,
and sad Ms Fletcher, we learned today,
likes building models with dominoes.
Mr Phipps can tell you what happened
in every episode of *Doctor Who*.
Mrs Sykes is an expert on dodos,
Mrs Major plays the kazoo.
But our deputy head, Mr McGuire,
must surely be strangest of all,
he likes to go out jogging
while carrying a cannonball!

(You think your teachers are weirder?
Well, here's a challenge for you,
just write their names and then list
the oddest things that they do . . .)

Brian Moses

* topiary – the art of cutting trees or bushes into odd shapes

61

Teachers' Playtime

It's wonderful being on duty
When the teachers come out to play
See them running and shouting and leaping about
On a sunny winter's day

62

But I have to send Mr Walton
Back to the class for his coat
Mrs Bateman's stayed in – there's a spot on her chin
(Her mother sent a note)

Mrs Croll hits Mr Pryor
She says he has stolen her ball
So I give her a lecture on sharing and caring
And I make her stand in the hall

Mrs Peck falls over and twists her foot
She's limping, but there's nothing to see
So I ask her to run to the staffroom
To fetch me a cup of tea

Miss Haylett's chasing Mr Griffiths
He's hiding in the boys' bog
He says he'll stay there all day if she won't go away
Cos she's trying to give him a snog

Mrs Rowlands, who works in the office
Does a handstand against the wall
You can see her navy-blue knickers
It's not very nice at all

I love it on playground duty
Bossing teachers still gives me a thrill
So I ring the bell two minutes early
And . . .

Mr Walton . . .

STAND STILL!

Roger Stevens (aged 10³⁄₄)

Mr Walton's on the Playground

Michael's ball is on the roof
And Darren's looking for a fight
Little Kelly Cupcake
Is dangling from her kite

But Mr Walton's on the playground
So everything will be all right

Noel went in the girls' loo
And gave the girls a fright
Yaseen won't let Gemma kiss him
But Derek Trubsall might

But Mr Walton's on the playground
So everything will be all right

Randeep's lost his pet rat
(He says it doesn't bite)
Michael says – Aren't people small
When viewed from this great height?

But Mr Walton's on the playground
So everything will be all right

Tommy's foot is swelling up
His laces are too tight
Now Michael's stuck up on the roof
He'll have to stay all night

But Mr Walton's on the playground
So everything will be er . . .

Where's Mr Walton gone?

Roger Stevens

64

Help!

Dear Mrs Berry
As you are our head teacher
I thought you should know
That I'm writing you this letter
On the floor under my table
Where I have accidentally on purpose
Dropped my pencil
I need to let you know quite urgently
That our supply teacher, Mr Pigge
Has gone mad. He ranted and raved at us
Using a lot of shouting and spit
Then he stapled Kieron to the wall
And tied Nicola to the door by her plaits
Now he's looking at me.

Whoops! Nearly got caught then!
Fortunately, when he threw his chair at me
I was still under the table
Sadly it hit the five kids next to me
Sent them flying I can tell you!
I can also report that Lucy
Has been glued to the floor for whispering
And Daniel, Gurteak and Sam
Were dumped in the bins by the boiler house
Jade, Sally and Lackveer are crying
And Josh has been shoved head first
Into the gerbil cage.

Hello Mrs Berry
I'm writing this from the cupboard where
Ten of us have been locked away
For writing notes in class.
I think Mr Pigge is asleep now
I can probably sneak this note
Through a crack in the back
Hoping that you will find it very quickly.
Please rescue us before home time
Unless it's maths homework tonight, in which case
Please leave us here till Monday.

Your friend Jack
In Year Five

David Harmer

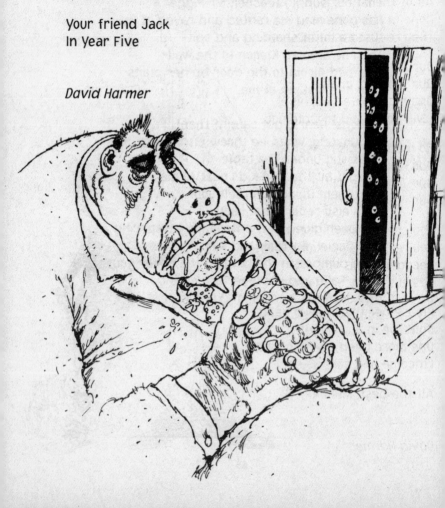

A Letter to the Teacher

Dear Teacher

Our Percy brought your note home
It says we must discuss
'His very bad behaviour'
What a lot of fuss!

I've got a lot of kids in school
All of them are good
None of them misbehave
They're just misunderstood.

Our Emma's in 4J
Our Tommy's in 3W
One more note like this
I will come and trouble you.

No more of this nonsense
Our Percy is a cutie
Our Tommy is a little star
Our Emma is a beauty.

You should know it's true
You're their favourite brother
Recognize this writing?
Yes, it's me, your mother.

Please get this in your head
Don't be in any doubt
One more peep from you, son
I'll come and sort you out . . .

All the best, Mum xxx

David Harmer

A Spell to Make the Headmaster's Trousers Fall Down During Assembly

When nobody can see you
Run backwards round the hall
Do this six times and six times more
To see those trousers fall
Spit upon your fingers
Rub them on your nose
Stick your left thumb in your right ear
Wiggle all your toes
Take ten rubber bands
And seven lengths of string
When the hall begins to fill
Softly start to sing.

Oh Headmaster, oh Headmaster
Your slacks are getting slacker
When this spell starts working
It will be a cracker
Your elasticated waistband
Will start to lose its grip
Your knobbly knees will feel the breeze
When those trousers slip.

Begin to cut the string
And snap the rubber bands
Cross your eyes, hold your breath
Clap with both your hands
Jump up and down, spin round and round
Shout 'Trousers, drop down quick'
Then the teachers and the children

Will see your magic trick
His trousers round his ankles
His spotty pants on view
Your poor red-faced headmaster
Just won't know what to do.

David Harmer

Our Teacher Is Really from Outer Space

Early morning he lands his spaceship
Behind the boilers where nobody goes
Then he wobbles across the yard
His bright purple hair glowing with sparks
His six eyes standing out on stalks
His fifteen arms ending in claws
His four mouths drooling orange spit.

Once inside he pops into the gents
Changes into his Earthling Teacher disguise
Hairy tweed jacket and scrawny tie
Saggy trousers with a shiny bottom
Squeaky shoes and the smell of chalk dust.

Sometimes in numeracy
He forgets where he is, starts scribbling
Strange signs and numbers across the board
Mutters and snorts in some weird language
His antennae nearly zoom up through his wig
His alien face peers through his mask.

In PE he sprouts ten legs
Does tricks with a football you wouldn't believe
And luckily for us, at dinner-time
He is a vegetarian.

After school when he thinks we can't see
He blasts off home to the faraway stars
With our homework under his arms
Just think, it could be
He has friends in lots of other schools.

Next time you're in assembly
Take a long look and try to guess
Which ones are the teachers from outer space.
They could be nearer than you think.

David Harmer

I've Seen Mrs Newton's Knickers

You'll never believe what I've seen!
Go on . . . have a guess
I've seen Mrs Newton's knickers
The pairs she wears beneath her dress.

Monday's pair is navy blue and thick
Because she teaches games.
Tuesday's science so they're fireproof
From the Bunsen burner's flames.

Wednesday she has lots of pairs
To add or take or share in maths.
Thursday's pair is waterproof
Because of swimming at the baths.

Friday's pair is vast, expansive,
Thermal, flannelette and so
Warming freezing playtime duties
They will reach from head to toe.

Wimbledon or tennis fortnight
Then they're white and rather frilly.
Do not look on April Fool's Day
Because they're very very silly.

Yellow spots, blue polka dots,
Tartan checks, deckchair stripes
But the most amazing pair
Is saved for raves on Saturday nights.

72

I've seen Mrs Newton's knickers
Every pattern, each design,
Every style in every colour
Hung up on her washing line!

Paul Cookson

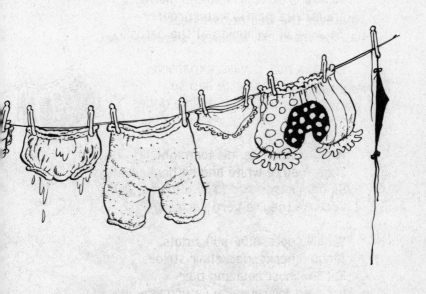

An Infant's Eye View of Teachers

Mr Knox has comedy socks
While Miss McHoots has rock-star boots

Mrs Hughes has sparkly shoes
See Mr Randall's open-toed sandals

Look at old Mrs Bright's old wrinkled tights
While young Mr Mortson always has short shorts on

The different stockings of young Miss Brockin
Are stripy, patterned and often shocking

Whatever the weather, Mr Heat
Has the cheesiest, stinkiest, sweatiest feet

Paul Cookson

Shhh!

Teacher's Pet

Teacher's pet isn't Billy
or Darren or Sharon or Lee
Teacher's pet isn't Sally
or Vicky or Nicky or me
Teacher's hunting for her pet
She's crawling around on all fours
Teacher's pet is a big black spider
and she keeps it in her drawers

Roger Stevens

75

Our Teacher

Our teacher taps his toes,
keeping the beat to some silent tune
only he knows.

Our teacher drums his fingers,
on his desk, on the window,
on anything, when the room is quiet,
when we're meant to be writing
in silence.

Our teacher cracks his knuckles,
clicks his fingers, grinds his teeth,
his knees are knocking the edge of his desk,
he breathes to a rhythmical beat.

When he turns his head in a certain way
there's a bone that cracks in his neck,
When he sinks to the floor
we often think he'll stay on his knees
for evermore, he's such a physical wreck!

Our teacher bangs his head against the wall,
(or pretends to) when Wendy comes up
with another dumb remark.

Our teacher says we annoy him
with all our silly fuss.
Perhaps he's never really thought
how much he irritates us.

Brian Moses

Sheep Wars: the Drama Teacher's Dilemma!

'We need more lines for Sheep 2 to say,
he doesn't say enough in our Nativity play.
His parents will complain if Sheep 2 is too dumb,
if they think his importance is less than Sheep 1.
They're the sort of parents who will time how long
Sheep 2 is on stage compared with Sheep 1,
and whether he's centre stage or sidelined,
then demand his position is redefined.

'So someone, please write more lines, and fast,
if Sheep 2's appearance on stage is to last
as long as Sheep 1 and then that will avoid
any trouble from his parents if they are annoyed . . .
The last thing we want is Sheep Wars to break out,
for the Sheepy parents to scream and shout.
This is, after all, the season of goodwill
so fill Sheep 2's mouth, let him speak until
the curtain comes down on our school play
and his parents, happy, lead him away.'

Brian Moses

Teacher's Desk

Teacher's desk

Elastic bands (confiscated)

A box of tissues

Cup of tea (cold)

Hanky (for runny noses)

Egg-boxes (useful)

Register

Sausage roll (half eaten)

Diary (last year's)

Elastoplasts (for cut knees)

Sellotape (used up)

Kind words (unlimited supply)

Roger Stevens

79

Not to Be Crossed (a sonnet)

She's big and wide but moves just like a cat
Along a wall. A smile like the queen.
Her choice of clothes is black. She wears a hat.
Although occasionally she will wear green.
She marks your book in pencil, never pen.
Her voice is quiet. As quiet as falling snow.
She very rarely rages. Now and then
Her voice raised. But does she shout? Oh no.
She fixes you with eyes as pale as a snake.
She stops you dead. She sees into your soul.
You cannot move. Your heart beats and you shake.
You want to shout, I'm sorry. Let me go!
Her class will tell you that she's kind and fair.
They never misbehave. They wouldn't dare.

Roger Stevens

SATs for Teachers

The teachers filed into the hall
their chatter was subdued
they found their places, settled down
at once their eyes were glued
to Ben and Rosie from Year Six
who called for their attention
the teachers soon sat up straight
fearing a detention
'You've got sharp pencils'
Rosie said 'And everything you need
so if you're ready sir and miss
now you may proceed'.

Say a man walked to Norwich
with a bucket full of water
he filled it up with fish and frogs
presents for his daughter
who sent him off to Sheringham
because the route was shorter
if he left at ten past three
what time would he have caught her?

Multiply five hundred pounds
by seven tenths of nine
add to it another twelve
then use a minus sign
to calculate the difference
between these sums of mine
add fifty more and ten again
and both your sums combine.

Now teachers you must write a book
full of force and power
and you have got for this task
just under half an hour
then tell me everything about
the inside of a flower
and the temperature of snow
when we have a shower.

The teachers looked quite baffled
upset, distraught, perplexed
these SATs were hard, impossible
it gave them all stiff necks
but Ben and Rosie laughed and laughed
at all these nervous wrecks
'Now you know what it's like'
they shouted 'So complex
we never understand a word
nothing much connects
and you've failed too, worse than us
and everyone expects
you to pass, go back to class
it's comprehension next'.

David Harmer

How Teachers Leave School Each Evening

The dance teacher floats down the stairway
and waltzes herself to the door.
Behind her the maths teacher counts every step
as he paces across the floor.

The geography teacher struggles to find
a different route home each night.
The PE teacher sets new daily records
for the swiftest homeward flight.

The English teacher recites to himself
lines of poetry by Keats.
The drama teacher's on camera,
a movie star in the streets.

85

The RE teacher prays
that there'll be no traffic queues.
The physics teacher knows there will
and regularly blows a fuse.

The IT teacher imagines he's left
as he follows some virtual route on screen.
It's a mystery why the history teacher
is met each night by a limousine.

Our music teacher, an Elvis freak,
plays air guitar along the drive.
With his rocker's quiff and Las Vegas suit
he's out there somewhere perfecting his jive.

But the teacher who's young and still keen
reluctantly closes the door,
ticks off the hours and minutes till she can be
back with her class once more.

Brian Moses

Teachers' Awards

At the end of each summer term
   amid much jollity and backslapping
Schoolteachers congratulate each other
   on surviving yet another school year.

So let's hear it for Mrs King,
   the queen of the big production number,
always on a short fuse,
   especially on duty days.

87

And not forgetting . . . Mr White
    for staying calm when the classroom radiator
leaked rusty water all over
    his recently completed pile of report cards.

Let's hear it for . . . Mrs Salmon,
    who restrained herself quite admirably
when the school gerbil
    ate her winning lottery ticket.

And for Mr Middleton, who has eaten school dinners
    for each day of his twenty-year career,
unable to be with us tonight,
    but we hope he'll be out of hospital soon.

And the romance of the year award
    goes to Miss Buchanan and Mr Duke,
they're dreadfully drippy when they're together,
    it really makes us . . . feel unwell!

And last of all, our dear headmaster,
    who led us all through good times and bad,
till our school inspection came along
    and he suddenly discovered
        a pressing engagement in Barbados.

So let's hear it for those
    fabulous, wonderful creatures,
where would you be without them?
    Let's hear it for THE TEACHERS . . .

Brian Moses

88

What Miss Did on Her Last Day in School

Ran down the corridors
Skateboarded in the dining hall
Sang pop songs in assembly
Ripped up all the SATs sheets

Flicked peas at the juniors
Danced on the tables
Skipped the most complicated skip
Scored the best goal at football

Slid down the banisters
Swung on the curtains
Brought her dog and seventeen cats
Let them loose in the kitchens

Made mud pies in the sandpit
Read a funny poem in literacy hour
Did impressions of the other teachers
Made the best paper planes ever

Gave us all sweets and a hug and a kiss
Cried when we sang her our goodbye song
Wiped our eyes when we cried with her
Told us she'd never forget us

Just like we will not forget her

Paul Cookson